THE COMPLETE POEMS

Stephen Crane

The Complete Poems

Honeycomb

The Complete Poems by Stephen Crane
is published by
Honeycomb Press
Dublin – New York
e-mail: honeycombpublishing@gmail.com
www.honeycombpress.webs.com

ISBN 978-1-4478-6863-7

Edited for Honeycomb by Anatoly Kudryavitsky.

All rights reserved.

Cover design © 2011 Honeycomb Press
Cover image: "Studien zweier Reiter" by Albrecht Dürer
Portrait of Stephen Crane by Corwin Knapp Linson (1894)

Printed in the United Kingdom

CONTENTS

Willa Cather. When I knew Stephen Crane   7

"Black Riders" (1895)   17

Uncollected Poems   89

"War is kind" (1899)   95

Poems Published Posthumously   137

Joseph Conrad. Stephen Crane   165

Index of First Lines   169

When I knew Stephen Crane

Willa Cather

It was, I think, in the spring of '94 that a slender, narrow-chested fellow in a shabby grey suit, with a soft felt hat pulled low over his eyes, sauntered into the office of the managing editor of the Nebraska State Journal and introduced himself as Stephen Crane. He stated that he was going to Mexico to do some work for the Bacheller Syndicate and get rid of his cough, and that he would be stopping in Lincoln for a few days. Later he explained that he was out of money and would be compelled to wait until he got a check from the East before he went further. I was a Junior at the Nebraska State University at the time, and was doing some work for the State Journal in my leisure time, and I happened to be in the managing editor's room when Mr. Crane introduced himself. I was just off the range; I knew a little Greek and something about cattle and a good horse when I saw one, and beyond horses and cattle I considered nothing of vital importance except good stories and the people who wrote them. This was the first man of letters I had ever met in the flesh, and when the young man announced who he was, I dropped into a chair behind the editor's desk where I could stare at him without being too much in evidence.

Only a very youthful enthusiasm and a large propensity for hero worship could have found anything impressive in the young man who stood before the managing editor's desk. He was thin to emaciation, his face was gaunt and unshaven, a thin dark moustache straggled on his upper lip, his black hair grew low on his forehead and was shaggy and unkempt. His grey clothes were much the worse for wear and fitted him so badly it seemed unlikely he had ever been measured for them. He wore a flannel shirt and a slovenly apology for a necktie, and his shoes were dusty and worn gray about the toes and were badly run over at the heel. I had seen many a tramp printer come up the Journal stairs to hunt a job, but never one who presented such a disreputable appearance as this story-maker man. He wore gloves, which seemed rather a contradiction to the general slovenliness of his attire, but when he took them off to search his pockets for his credentials, I noticed that his hands were singularly fine; long, white, and delicately shaped, with thin, nervous fingers. I have seen pictures of Aubrey Beardsley's hands that recalled Crane's very vividly.

At that time Crane was but twenty-four, and almost an unknown man. Hamlin Garland had seen some of his work and believed in him, and had introduced him to Mr. Howells, who recommended him to the Bacheller Syndicate. "The Red Badge of Courage" had been published in the State Journal that winter along with a lot of other syndicate matter, and the grammatical construction of the story was so faulty that the managing editor had several times called on me to edit the copy. In this way I had read it very carefully, and through the careless sentence-structure I saw the wonder of that remarkable performance. But the grammar certainly was bad. I remember one of the reporters who had corrected the phrase "it don't" for the tenth time remarked savagely, "If I couldn't write better English than this, I'd quit."

Crane spent several days in the town, living from hand to mouth and waiting for his money. I think he borrowed a small amount from the managing editor. He lounged about the office most of the time, and I frequently encountered him going in and out of the cheap restaurants on Tenth Street. When he was at the office he talked a good deal in a wandering, absent-minded fashion, and his conversation was uniformly frivolous. If he could not evade a serious question by a joke, he bolted. I cut my classes to lie in wait for him, confident that in some unwary moment I could trap him into serious conversation, that if one burned incense long enough and ardently enough, the oracle would not be dumb. I was Maupassant mad at the time, a malady particularly unattractive in a Junior, and I made a frantic effort to get an expression of opinion from him on "Le Bonheur". "Oh, you're Moping, are you?" he remarked with a sarcastic grin, and went on reading a little volume of Poe that he carried in his pocket. At another time I cornered him in the Funny Man's room and succeeded in getting a little out of him. We were taught literature by an exceedingly analytical method at the University, and we probably distorted the method, and I was busy trying to find the least common multiple of "Hamlet" and the greatest common divisor of "Macbeth", and I began asking him whether stories were constructed by cabalistic formulae. At length he sighed wearily and shook his drooping shoulders, remarking:

"Where did you get all that rot? Yarns aren't done by mathematics. You can't do it by rule any more than you can dance by rule. You have to have the itch of the thing in your fingers, and if you haven't, – well, you're damned lucky, and you'll live long and prosper, that's all." – And with that he yawned and went down the hall.

Crane was moody most of the time, his health was bad and he seemed profoundly discouraged. Even his jokes were exceedingly drastic. He went about with the tense, preoccupied, self-centered air of a man who is brooding over some impending disaster, and I conjectured vainly as to what it might be. Though he was seemingly entirely idle during the few days I knew him, his manner indicated that he was in the throes of work that told terribly on his nerves. His eyes I remember as the finest I have ever seen, large and dark and full of lustre and changing lights, but with a profound melancholy always lurking deep in them. They were eyes that seemed to be burning themselves out.

As he sat at the desk with his shoulders drooping forward, his head low, and his long, white fingers drumming on the sheets of copy paper, he was as nervous as a race horse fretting to be on the track. Always, as he came and went about the halls, he seemed like a man preparing for a sudden departure. Now that he is dead it occurs to me that all his life was a preparation for sudden departure. I remember once when he was writing a letter he stopped and asked me about the spelling of a word, saying carelessly, "I haven't time to learn to spell."

Then, glancing down at his attire, he added with an absent-minded smile, "I haven't time to dress either; it takes an awful slice out of a fellow's life."

He said he was poor, and he certainly looked it, but four years later when he was in Cuba, drawing the largest salary ever paid a newspaper correspondent, he clung to this same untidy manner of dress, and his ragged overalls and buttonless shirt were eyesores to the immaculate Mr. Davis, in his spotless linen and neat khaki uniform, with his Gibson chin always freshly shaven. When I first heard of his serious illness, his old throat trouble aggravated into consumption by his reckless exposure in Cuba, I recalled a passage from Maeterlinck's essay, "The Pre-Destined," on those doomed to early death: "As children, life seems nearer to them than to other children. They appear to know nothing, and yet there is in their eyes so profound a certainty that we feel they must know all. – In all haste, but wisely and with minute care do they prepare themselves to live, and this very haste is a sign upon which mothers can scarce bring themselves to look." I remembered, too, the young man's melancholy and his tenseness, his burning eyes, and his way of slurring over the less important things, as one whose time is short.

I have heard other people say how difficult it was to induce Crane to talk seriously about his work, and I suspect that he was particularly averse to discussions with literary men of wider education and better equipment than himself, yet he seemed to feel that this fuller culture was not for him. Perhaps the unreasoning instinct which lies deep in the roots of our lives, and which guides us all, told him that he had not time enough to acquire it.

Men will sometimes reveal themselves to children, or to people whom they think never to see again, more completely than they ever do to their confreres. From the wise we hold back alike our folly and our wisdom, and for the recipients of our deeper confidences we seldom select our equals. The soul has no message for the friends with whom we dine every week. It is silenced by custom and convention, and we play only in the shallows. It selects its listeners willfully, and seemingly delights to waste its best upon the chance wayfarer who meets us in the highway at a fated hour. There are moments too, when the tides run high or very low, when self-revelation is necessary to every man, if it be only to his valet or his gardener. At such a moment, I was with Mr. Crane.

The hoped for revelation came unexpectedly enough. It was on the last night he spent in Lincoln. I had come back from the theatre and was in the Journal office writing a notice of the play. It was eleven o'clock when Crane came in. He had expected his money to arrive on the night mail and it had not done so, and he was out of sorts and deeply despondent. He sat down on the ledge of the open window that faced on the street, and when I had finished my notice I went over and took a chair beside him. Quite without invitation on my part, Crane began to talk, began to curse his trade from the first throb of creative desire in a boy to the finished work of the master. The night was oppressively warm; one of those dry winds that are the curse of that country was blowing up from Kansas. The white, western moonlight threw sharp, blue shadows below us. The streets were silent at that hour, and we could hear the gurgle of the fountain in the Post Office square across the street, and the twang of banjos from the lower verandah of the Hotel Lincoln, where the colored waiters were serenading the guests. The drop lights in the office were dull under their green shades, and the telegraph sounder clicked faintly in the next room. In all his long tirade, Crane never raised his voice; he spoke slowly and monotonously and even calmly, but I have never known so bitter a heart in any man as he revealed to me that night. It was an arraignment of the wages of life, an invocation to the ministers of hate.

Incidentally he told me the sum he had received for "The Red Badge of Courage", which I think was something like ninety dollars, and he repeated some lines from "The Black Riders", which was then in preparation. He gave me to understand that he led a double literary life; writing in the first place the matter that pleased himself, and doing it very slowly; in the second place, any sort of stuff that would sell. And he remarked that his poor was just as bad as it could possibly be.

He realized, he said, that his limitations were absolutely impassable. "What I can't do, I can't do at all, and I can't acquire it. I only hold one trump."

He had no settled plans at all. He was going to Mexico wholly uncertain of being able to do any successful work there, and he seemed to feel very insecure about the financial end of his venture. The thing that most interested me was what he said about his slow method of composition. He declared that there was little money in story-writing at best, and practically none in it for him, because of the time it took him to work up his detail. Other men, he said, could sit down and write up an experience while the physical effect of it, so to speak, was still upon them, and yesterday's impressions made to-day's "copy." But when he came in from the streets to write up what he had seen there, his faculties were benumbed, and he sat twirling his pencil and hunting for words like a schoolboy.

I mentioned "The Red Badge of Courage", which was written in nine days, and he replied that, though the writing took very little time, he had been unconsciously working the detail of the story out through most of his boyhood. His ancestors had been soldiers, and he had been imagining war stories ever since he was out of knickerbockers, and in writing his first war story he had simply gone over his imaginary campaigns and selected his favorite imaginary experiences. He declared that his imagination was hide bound; it was there, but it pulled hard. After he got a notion for a story, months passed before he could get any sort of personal contract with it, or feel any potency to handle it. "The detail of a thing has to filter through my blood, and then it comes out like a native product, but it takes forever," he remarked. I distinctly remember the illustration, for it rather took hold of me.

I have often been astonished since to hear Crane spoken of as "the reporter in fiction", for the reportorial faculty of superficial reception and quick transference was what he conspicuously lacked. His first newspaper account of his shipwreck on the filibuster "Commodore" off the Florida coast was as lifeless as the "copy" of a police court reporter. It was many months afterwards that the literary product of his terrible experience appeared in that marvelous sea story "The Open Boat", unsurpassed in its vividness and constructive perfection.

At the close of our long conversation that night, when the copy boy came in to take me home, I suggested to Crane that in ten years he would probably laugh at all his temporary discomfort. Again his body took on that strenuous tension and he clenched his hands, saying, "I can't wait ten years, I haven't time."

The ten years are not up yet, and he has done his work and gathered his reward and gone. Was ever so much experience and achievement crowded into so short a space of time? A great man dead at twenty-nine! That would have puzzled the ancients. Edward Garnett wrote of him in The Academy of December 17, 1899: "I cannot remember a parallel in the literary history of fiction. Maupassant, Meredith, Henry James, Mr. Howells and Tolstoy, were all learning their expression at an age where Crane had achieved his and achieved it triumphantly." He had the precocity of those doomed to die in youth. I am convinced that when I met him he had a vague premonition of the shortness of his working day, and in the heart of the man there was that which said, "That thou doest, do quickly."

At twenty-one this son of an obscure New Jersey rector, with but a scant reading knowledge of French and no training, had rivaled in technique the foremost craftsmen of the Latin races. In the six years since I met him, a stranded reporter, he stood in the firing line during two wars, knew hairbreadth 'scapes on land and sea, and established himself as the first writer of his time in the picturing of episodic, fragmentary life. His friends have charged him with fickleness, but he was a man who was in the preoccupation of haste. He went from country to country, from man to man, absorbing all that was in them for him. He had no time to look backward. He had no leisure for "camaraderie". He drank life to the lees, but at the banquet table where other men took their ease and jested over their wine, he stood a dark and silent figure, sombre as Poe himself, not wishing to be understood; and he took his portion in haste, with his loins girded, and his shoes on his feet, and his staff in his hand, like one who must depart quickly.

First published in *The Library*, June 23, 1900

Black Riders
(1895)

- 1 -

Black Riders came from the sea.
There was clang and clang of spear and shield,
And clash and clash of hoof and heel,
Wild shouts and the wave of hair
In the rush upon the wind:
Thus the ride of Sin.

Three little birds in a row
Sat musing.
A man passed near that place.
Then did the little birds nudge each other.

They said: "He thinks he can sing".
They threw back their heads to laugh.
With quaint countenances
They regarded him.
They were very curious,
Those three little birds in a row.

- 3 -

In the desert
I saw a creature, naked, bestial,
Who, squatting upon the ground,
Held his heart in his hands,
And ate of it.
I said: "Is it good, friend?"
"It is bitter – bitter," he answered;
"But I like it
Because it is bitter,
And because it is my heart."

- 4 -

Yes, I have a thousand tongues,
And nine and ninety-nine lie.
Though I strive to use the one,
It will make no melody at my will,
But is dead in my mouth.

- 5 -

Once there came a man
Who said:
"Range me all men of the world in rows."
And instantly
There was terrific clamor among the people
Against being ranged in rows.
There was a loud quarrel, world-wide.
It endured for ages;
And blood was shed
By those who would not stand in rows,
And by those who pined to stand in rows.
Eventually, the man went to death, weeping.
And those who stayed in bloody scuffle
Knew not great simplicity.

- 6 -

God fashioned the ship of the world carefully.
With the infinite skill of an All-Master
Made He the hull and the sails,
Held He the rudder
Ready for adjustment.
Erect stood He, scanning His work proudly.
Then – at fateful time – a Wrong called,
And God turned, heeding.
Lo, the ship, at this opportunity, slipped slyly,
Making cunning noiseless travel down the ways.
So that, forever rudderless, it went upon the seas
Going ridiculous voyages,
Making quaint progress,
Turning as with serious purpose
Before stupid winds.
And there were many in the sky
Who laughed at this thing.

- 7 -

Mystic Shadow, bending near me,
Who art thou?
Whence come ye?
And – tell me – is it fair
Or is the truth bitter as eaten fire?
Tell me!
Fear not that I should quaver,
For I dare – I dare.
Then, tell me!

- 8 -

I looked here;
I looked there;
Nowhere could I see my love.
And – this time –
She was in my heart.
Truly, then, I have no complaint,
For though she be fair and fairer,
She is none so fair as she
In my heart.

- 9 -

I stood upon a high place,
And saw, below, many devils
Running, leaping.
And carousing in sin.
One looked up, grinning,
And said: "Comrade! Brother!"

- 10 -

Should the wide world roll away,
Leaving black terror,
Limitless night,
Nor God, nor man, nor place to stand
Would be to me essential,
If thou and thy white arms were there,
And the fall to doom a long way.

- 11 -

In a lonely place,
I encountered a sage
Who sat, all still,
Regarding a newspaper.
He accosted me:
"Sir, what is this?"
Then I saw that I was greater,
Aye, greater than this sage.
I answered him at once:
"Old, old man, it is the wisdom of the age."
The sage looked upon me with admiration.

- 12 -

"And the sins of the fathers shall be visited upon the heads of the children, even unto the third and fourth generation of them that hate me."

Well, then, I hate thee, Unrighteous Picture;
Wicked Image, I hate thee;
So, strike with thy vengeance
The heads of those little men
Who come blindly.
It will be a brave thing.

- 13 -

If there is a witness to my little life,
To my tiny throes and struggles,
He sees a fool;
And it is not fine for gods to menace fools.

- 14 -

There was crimson clash of war.
Lands turned black and bare;
Women wept;
Babes ran, wondering.
There came one who understood not these things.
He said: "Why is this?"
Whereupon a million strove to answer him.
There was such intricate clamor of tongues,
That still the reason was not.

- 15 -

"Tell brave deeds of war."

Then they recounted tales:
"There were stern stands
And bitter runs for glory."

Ah, I think there were braver deeds.

- 16 -

Charity, thou art a lie,
A toy of women,
A pleasure of certain men.
In the presence of justice,
Lo, the walls of the temple
Are visible
Through thy form of sudden shadows.

- 17 -

There were many who went in huddled procession,
They knew not whither;
But, at any rate, success or calamity
Would attend all in equality.

There was one who sought a new road.
He went into direful thickets,
And ultimately he died thus, alone;
But they said he had courage.

- 18 -

In Heaven,
Some little blades of grass
Stood before God.
"What did you do?"
Then all save one of the little blades
Began eagerly to relate
The merits of their lives.
This one stayed a small way behind,
Ashamed.
Presently, God said:
"And what did you do?"
The little blade answered: "Oh, my Lord,
Memory is bitter to me,
For, if I did good deeds,
I know not of them."
Then God, in all His splendor,
Arose from His throne.
"Oh, best little blade of grass!" He said.

- 19 -

A god in wrath
Was beating a man;
He cuffed him loudly
With thunderous blows
That rang and rolled over the earth.
All people came running.
The man screamed and struggled,
And bit madly at the feet of the god.
The people cried:
"Ah, what a wicked man!"
And –
"Ah, what a redoubtable god!"

- 20 -

A learned man came to me once.
He said: "I know the way, – come."
And I was overjoyed at this.
Together we hastened.
Soon, too soon, were we
Where my eyes were useless,
And I knew not the ways of my feet.
I clung to the hand of my friend;
But at last he cried: "I am lost."

- 21 -

There was, before me,
Mile upon mile
Of snow, ice, burning sand.
And yet I could look beyond all this,
To a place of infinite beauty;
And I could see the loveliness of her
Who walked in the shade of the trees.
When I gazed,
All was lost
But this place of beauty and her.
When I gazed.
And in my gazing, desired,
Then came again
Mile upon mile,
Of snow, ice, burning sand.

- 22 -

Once I saw Mountains angry,
And ranged in battle-front.
Against them stood a little man;
Aye, he was no bigger than my finger.
I laughed, and spoke to one near me:
"Will he prevail?"
"Surely," replied this other;
"His grandfathers beat them many times."
Then did I see much virtue in grandfathers, –
At least, for the little man
Who stood against the Mountains.

- 23 -

Places among the stars,
Soft gardens near the sun,
Keep your distant beauty;
Shed no beams upon my weak heart.
Since she is here
In a place of blackness,
Not your golden days
Nor your silver nights
Can call me to you.
Since she is here
In a place of blackness,
Here I stay and wait.

- 24 -

I saw a man pursuing the horizon;
Round and round they sped.
I was disturbed at this;
I accosted the man.
"It is futile," I said,
"You can never —"

"You lie," he cried,
And ran on.

- 25 -

Behold, the grave of a wicked man,
And near it, a stern spirit.

There came a drooping maid with violets,
But the spirit grasped her arm.
"No flowers for him," he said.
The maid wept:
"Ah, I loved him."
But the spirit, grim and frowning;
"No flowers for him."

Now, this is it —
If the spirit was just,
Why did the maid weep?

- 26 -

There was set before me a mighty hill,
And long days I climbed
Through regions of snow.
When I had before me the summit-view,
It seemed that my labor
Had been to see gardens
Lying at impossible distances.

- 27 -

A youth in apparel that glittered
Went to walk in a grim forest.
There he met an assassin
Attired all in garb of old days;
He, scowling through the thickets,
And dagger poised quivering.
Rushed upon the youth.
"Sir," said this latter,
"I am enchanted, believe me,
To die, thus,
In this medieval fashion,
According to the best legends;
Ah, what joy!"
Then took he the wound, smiling,
And died, content.

- 28 -

"Truth," said a traveller,
"Is a rock, a mighty fortress;
Often have I been to it,
Even to its highest tower,
From whence the world looks black."

"Truth," said a traveller,
"Is a breath, a wind,
A shadow, a phantom;
Long have I pursued it,
But never have I touched
The hem of its garment."

And I believed the second traveller;
For truth was to me
A breath, a wind,
A shadow, a phantom,
And never had I touched
The hem of its garment.

- 29 -

Behold, from the land of the farther suns
I returned.
And I was in a reptile-swarming place,
Peopled, otherwise, with grimaces,
Shrouded above in black impenetrableness.
I shrank, loathing.
Sick with it.
And I said to him:
"What is this?"
He made answer slowly:
"Spirit, this is a world;
This was your home."

- 30 -

Supposing that I should have the courage
To let a red sword of virtue
Plunge into my heart,
Letting to the weeds of the ground
My sinful blood,
What can you offer me?
A gardened castle?
A flowery kingdom?

What? A hope?
Then hence with your red sword of virtue.

- 31 -

Many workmen
Built a huge ball of masonry
Upon a mountain-top.
Then they went to the valley below,
And turned to behold their work.
"It is grand," they said;
They loved the thing.

Of a sudden, it moved:
It came upon them swiftly;
It crushed them all to blood.
But some had opportunity to squeal.

- 32 -

Two or three angels
Came near to the earth.
They saw a fat church.
Little black streams of people
Came and went in continually.
And the angels were puzzled
To know why the people went thus,
And why they stayed so long within.

- 33 -

There was one I met upon the road
Who looked at me with kind eyes.
He said: "Show me of your wares."
And I did,
Holding forth one.
He said: "It is a sin."
Then I held forth another.
He said: "It is a sin."
Then I held forth another.
He said: "It is a sin."
And so to the end.
Always He said: "It is a sin."
At last, I cried out:
"But I have none other."
He looked at me
With kinder eyes.
"Poor soul," He said.

- 34 -

I stood upon a highway,
And, behold, there came
Many strange pedlers.
To me each one made gestures,
Holding forth little images, saying;
"This is my pattern of God.
Now this is the God I prefer."

But I said: "Hence!
Leave me with mine own,
And take you yours away;
I can't buy of your patterns of Cod,
The little Gods you may rightly prefer."

- 35 -

A man saw a ball of gold in the sky,
He climbed for it,
And eventually he achieved it –
It was clay.

Now this is the strange part:
When the man went to the earth
And looked again,
Lo, there was the ball of gold.
Now this is the strange part:
It was a ball of gold.
Aye, by the heavens, it was a ball of gold.

I met a seer.
He held in his hands
The book of wisdom.
"Sir," I addressed him,
"Let me read."
"Child –" he began.
"Sir," I said,
"Think not that I am a child,
For already I know much
Of that which you hold.
Aye, much."

He smiled.
Then he opened the book
And held it before me. –
Strange that I should have grown so suddenly blind.

- 37 -

On the horizon the peaks assembled;
And as I looked,
The march of the mountains began.
As they marched, they sang:
"Aye! We come! We come!"

- 38 -

The ocean said to me once:
"Look!
Yonder on the shore
Is a woman, weeping.
I have watched her.
Go you and tell her this, —
Her lover I have laid
In cool green hall.
There is wealth of golden sand
And pillars, coral-red;
Two white fish stand guard at his bier.

"Tell her this
And more, —
That the king of the seas
Weeps too, old, helpless man.
The bustling fates
Heap his hands with corpses
Until he stands like a child
With surplus of toys."

- 39 -

The livid lightnings flashed in the clouds;
The leaden thunders crashed.
A worshipper raised his arm.
"Hearken! Hearken! The voice of God!"

"Not so," said a man.
"The voice of God whispers in the heart
So softly
That the soul pauses,
Making no noise,
And strives for these melodies,
Distant, sighing, like faintest breath,
And all the being is still to hear."

- 40 -

And you love me?

I love you.

You are, then, cold coward.

Aye; but, beloved,
When I strive to come to you,
Man's opinions, a thousand thickets,
My interwoven existence,
My life,
Caught in the stubble of the world
Like a tender veil, –
This stays me.
No strange move can I make
Without noise of tearing.
I dare not.

If love loves,
There is no world
Nor word.
All is lost
Save thought of love
And place to dream.
You love me?

I love you.
You are, then, cold coward.
Aye; but, beloved –

- 41 -

Love walked alone.
The rocks cut her tender feet,
And the brambles tore her fair limbs.
There came a companion to her,
But, alas, he was no help,
For his name was Heart's Pain.

- 42 -

I walked in a desert.
And I cried:
"Ah, God, take me from this place!"
A voice said: "It is no desert."
I cried: "Well, but —
The sand, the heat, the vacant horizon."
A voice said: "It is no desert."

- 43 -

There came whisperings in the winds:
"Good-bye! Good-bye!"
Little voices called in the darkness:
"Good-bye! Good-bye!"
Then I stretched forth my arms.
"No – No –"
There came whisperings in the wind:
"Good-bye! Good-bye!"
Little voices called in the darkness:
"Good-bye! Good-bye!"

- 44 -

I was in the darkness;
I could not see my words
Nor the wishes of my heart.
Then suddenly there was a great light –

"Let me into the darkness again."

- 45 -

Tradition, thou art for suckling children.
Thou art the enlivening milk for babes;
But no meat for men is in thee.
Then –
But, alas, we all are babes.

- 46 -

Many red devils ran from my heart
And out upon the page.
They were so tiny
The pen could mash them.
And many struggled in the ink.
It was strange
To write in this red muck
Of things from my heart.

- 47 -

"Think as I think," said a man,
"Or you are abominably wicked,
You are a toad."

And after I had thought of it,
I said: "I will, then, be a toad".

- 48 -

Once there was a man, –
Oh, so wise!
In all drink
He detected the bitter,
And in all touch
He found the sting.
At last he cried thus:
"There is nothing, –
No life,
No joy,
No pain, –
There is nothing save opinion,
And opinion be damned."

- 49 -

I stood musing in a black world,
Not knowing where to direct my feel.
And I saw the quick stream of men
Pouring ceaselessly,
Filled with eager faces,
A torrent of desire.
I called to them:
"Where do you go? What do you see?"
A thousand voices called to me.
A thousand fingers pointed.
"Look! Look! There!"

I know not of it.
But, lo! in the far shy shone a radiance
Ineffable, divine, –
A vision painted upon a pall;
And sometimes was,
And sometimes it was not.
I hesitated.
Then from the stream
Came roaring voices,
Impatient:
"Look! Look! There!"

So again I saw,
And leaped, unhesitant,
And struggled and fumed
With outspread clutching fingers.
The hard hills tore my flesh;
The ways bit my feet.
At last I looked again.

No radiance in the far sky,
Ineffable, divine,
No vision painted upon a pall;
And always my eyes ached for the light.
Then I cried in despair:
"I see nothing! Oh, where do I go?"
The torrent turned again its faces:
"Look! Look! There!"
And at the blindness of my spirit
They screamed:
"Fool! Fool! Fool!"

- 50 -

You say you are holy,
And that
Because I have not seen you sin.
Aye, but there are those
Who see you sin, my friend.

- 51 -

A man went before a strange god, –
The god of many men, sadly wise.
And the deity thundered loudly,
Fat with rage, and puffing:
"Kneel, mortal, and cringe
And grovel and do homage
To my particularly sublime majesty."

    The man fled.

Then the man went to another god, –
The god of his inner thoughts.
And this one looked at him
With soft eyes
Lit with infinite comprehension,
And said: "My poor child!"

- 52 -

Why do you strive for greatness, fool?
Go pluck a bough and wear it.
It is as sufficing.

My Lord, there are certain barbarians
Who tilt their noses
As if the stars were flowers,
And thy servant is lost among their shoe-buckles.
Fain would I have mine eyes even with their eyes.

Fool, go pluck a bough and wear it.

- 53 -

I
Blustering god,
Stamping across the sky
With loud swagger,
I fear you not.
No, though from your highest heaven
You plunge your spear at my heart,
I fear you not.
No, not if the blow
Is as the lightning blasting tree,
I fear you not, puffing braggart.

II
If thou can see into my heart
That I fear thee not,
Thou wilt see why I fear thee not,
And why it is right.
So threaten not, thou, with thy bloody spears,
Else thy sublime ears shall hear curses.

III
Withal, there is one whom I fear;
I fear to see grief upon that face.
Perchance, friend, he is not your god;
If so, spit upon him.
By it you will do no profanity.
But I –
Ah, sooner would I die
Than see tears in those eyes of my soul.

- 54 -

"It was wrong to do this," said the angel
"You should live like a flower,
Holding malice like a puppy,
Waging war like a lambkin."

"Not so," quoth the man
Who had no fear of spirits;
"It is only wrong for angels
Who can live like the flowers,
Holding malice like the puppies,
Waging war like the lambkins."

- 55 -

A man toiled on a burning road,
Never resting.
Once he saw a fat, stupid ass
Grinning at him from a green place.
The man cried out in rage:
"Ah! do not deride me, fool!
I know you –
All day stuffing your belly,
Burying your heart
In grass and tender sprouts:
It will not suffice you."
But the ass only grinned at him from the green place.

- 56 -

A man feared that he might find an assassin,
Another that he might find a victim.
One was more wise than the other.

- 57 -

With eye and with gesture
You say you are holy.
I say you lie;
For I did see you
Draw away your coals
From the sin upon the hands
Of a little child.
Liar!

- 58 -

The sage lectured brilliantly.
Before him, two images:
"Now this one is a devil,
And this one is me."
He turned away.
Then a cunning pupil
Changed the positions.
Turned the sage again:
"Now this one is a devil,
And this one is me."
The pupils sat, all grinning,
And rejoiced in the game.
But the sage was a sage.

- 59 -

Walking in the sky,
A man in strange black garb
Encountered a radiant form.
Then his steps were eager;
Bowed he devoutly.
"My Lord," said he.
But the spirit knew him not.

- 60 -

Upon the road of my life,
Passed me many fair creatures,
Clothed all in white, and radiant.
To one, finally, I made speech:
"Who art thou?"
But she, like the others,
Kept cowled her face,
And answered in haste, anxiously:
"I am Good Deed, forsooth;
You have often seen me."
"Not uncowled," I made reply.
And with rash and strong hand,
Though she resisted,
I drew away the veil
And gazed at the features of Vanity.
She, shamefaced, went on;
And after I had mused a time,
I said of myself:
     "Fool!"

- 61 -

I
There was a man and a woman
Who sinned.
Then did the man heap the punishment
All upon the head of her,
And went away gayly.

II
There was a man and a woman
Who sinned.
And the man stood with her.
As upon her head, so upon his,
Fell blow and blow,
And all people screaming: "Fool!"
He was a brave heart.

III
He was a brave heart.
Would you speak with him, friend?
Well, he is dead,
And there went your opportunity.
Let it be your grief
That he is dead
And your opportunity gone;
For, in that, you were a coward.

- 62 -

There was a man who lived a life of fire.
Even upon the fabric of time,
Where purple becomes orange
And orange purple,
This life glowed,
A dire red slain, indelible;
Yet when he was dead,
He saw that he had not lived.

- 63 -

There was a great cathedral.
To solemn song,
A white procession
Moved toward the altar.
The chief man there
Was erect, and bore himself proudly.
Yet some could see him cringe,
As in a place of danger,
Throwing frightened glances into the air,
A-start at threatening faces of the past.

- 64 -

Friend, your white beard sweeps the ground.
Why do you stand, expectant?
Do you hope to see it
In one of your withered days?
With your old eyes
Do you hope to see
The triumphal march of Justice?
Do not wait, friend!
Take your white beard
And your old eyes
To more tender lands.

- 65 -

Once, I knew a fine song,
– It is true, believe me, –
It was all of birds,
And I held them in a basket;
When I opened the wicket,
Heavens! they all flew away.
I cried: "Come back little thoughts!"
But they only laughed.
They flew on
Until they were as sand
Thrown between me and the sky.

- 66 -

If I should cast off this tattered coal,
And go free into the mighty sky;
If I should find nothing there
But a vast blue,
Echoless, ignorant, –
What then?

- 67 -

God lay dead in Heaven;
Angels sang the hymn of the end;
Purple winds went moaning,
Their wings drip-dripping
With blood
That fell upon the earth.
It, groaning thing,
Turned black and sank.
Then from the far caverns
Of dead sins
Came monsters, livid with desire.
They fought,
Wrangled over the world,
A morsel.
But of all sadness this was sad, –
A woman's arms tried to shield
The head of a sleeping man
From the jaws of the final beast.

- 68 -

A spirit sped
Through spaces of night;
And as he sped, he called:
"God! God!"
He went through valleys
Of black death-slime,
Ever calling:
"God! God!"
Their echoes
From crevice and cavern
Mocked him:
"God! God! God!"
Fleetly into the plains of space
He went, ever calling:
"God! God!"
Eventually, then, he screamed,
Mad in denial:
"Ah, there is no God!"

A swift hand,
A sword from the sky,
Smote him,
And he was dead.

Uncollected Poems

Legends

I
A man builded a bugle for the storms to blow.
The focused winds hurled him afar.
He said that the instrument was a failure.

II
When the suicide arrived at the sky, the people
   there asked him: "Why?"
He replied: "Because no one admired me."

III
A man said: "Thou tree!"
The tree answered with the same scorn: "Thou man!
Thou art greater than I only in thy possibilities."

IV
A warrior stood upon a peak and defied the stars.
A little magpie, happening there, desired the
   soldier's plume, and so plucked it.

V
The wind that waves the blossoms sang, sang, sang
   from age to age.
The flowers were made curious by this joy.
"Oh, wind," they said, "why sing you at your
   labour, while we, pink beneficiaries, sing
   not, but idle, idle, idle from age to age?"

- 74 -

When a people reach the top of a hill
Then does God lean toward them,
Shortens tongues, lengthens arms.
A vision of their dead comes to the weak.
The moon shall not be too old
Before the new battalions rise
      – Blue battalions –
The moon shall not be too old
When the children of change shall fall
Before the new battalions
      – The blue battalions –

Mistakes and virtues will be trampled deep
A church a thief shall fall together
A sword will come at the bidding of the eyeless,
The God-led, turning only to beckon.
Swinging a creed like a censer
At the head of the new battalions
      – Blue battalions –
March the tools of nature's impulse
Men born of wrong, men born of right
Men of the new battalions
      – The blue battalions –

The clang of swords is Thy wisdom
The wounded make gestures like Thy Son's
The feet of mad horses is one part,
– Aye, another is the hand of a mother
on the brow of a son.
Then swift as they charge through a shadow.
The men of the new battalions

         – Blue battalions –
God lead them high. God lead them far
Lead them far, lead them high
These new battalions
         – The blue battalions –

- 75 -

Rumbling, buzzing, turning, whirling Wheels,
Dizzy Wheels!
Wheels!

War is Kind
(1899)

Do not weep, maiden, for war is kind.
Because your lover threw wild hands toward the sky
And the affrighted steed ran on alone,
Do not weep.
War is kind.

   Hoarse, booming drums of the regiment,
   Little souls who thirst for fight,
   These men were born to drill and die.
   The unexplained glory flies above them,
   Great is the Battle-God, great, and his Kingdom –
   A field where a thousand corpses lie.

Do not weep, babe, for war is kind.
Because your father tumbled in the yellow trenches,
Raged at his breast, gulped and died,
Do not weep.
War is kind.

   Swift blazing flag of the regiment,
   Eagle with crest of red and gold,
   These men were born to drill and die.
   Point for them the virtue of slaughter,
   Make plain to them the excellence of killing
   And a field where a thousand corpses lie.

Mother whose heart hung humble as a button
On the bright splendid shroud of your son,
Do not weep.
War is kind.

"What says the sea, little shell?
What says the sea?
Long has our brother been silent to us,
Kept his message for the ships,
Awkward ships, stupid ships."

"The sea bids you mourn, oh, pines,
Sing low in the moonlight.
He sends tale of the land of doom,
Of place where endless falls
A rain of women's tears,
And men in grey robes —
Men in grey robes —
Chant the unknown pain."

"What says the sea, little shell?
What says the sea?
Long has our brother been silent to us,
Kept his message for the ships,
Puny ships, silly ships."

"The sea bids you teach, oh, pines,
Sing low in the moonlight,
Teach the gold of patience,
Cry gospel of gentle hands,
Cry a brotherhood of hearts.
The sea bids you teach, oh, pines."

"And where is the reward, little shell?
What says the sea?
Long has our brother been silent to us,
Kept his message for the ships,

Puny ships, silly ships."

"No word says the sea, oh, pines,
No word says the sea.
Long will your brother be silent to you,
Keep his message for the ships,
Oh, puny pines, silly pines."

- 78 -

To the maiden
The sea was blue meadow
Alive with little froth-people
Singing.

To the sailor, wrecked,
The sea was dead grey walls
Superlative in vacancy
Upon which nevertheless at fateful time
Was written
The grim hatred of nature.

- 79 -

A little ink more or less!
It surely can't matter?
Even the sky and the opulent sea,
The plains and the hills, aloof,
Hear the uproar of all these books.
But it is only a little ink more or less.

What?
You define me God with these trinkets?
Can my misery meal on an ordered walking
Of surpliced numbskulls?
And a fanfare of lights?
Or even upon the measured pulpitings
Of the familiar false and true?
Is this God?
Where, then, is hell?
Show me some bastard mushroom
Sprung from a pollution of blood.
It is better.

Where is God?

- 80 -

"Have you ever made a just man?"
"Oh, I have made three," answered God,
"But two of them are dead
And the third –
Listen! Listen!
And you will hear the third of his defeat."

- 81 -

I explain the silvered passing of a ship at night,
The sweep of each sad lost wave
The dwindling boom of the steel thing's striving
The little cry of a man to a man
A shadow falling across the greyer night
And the sinking of the small star.

Then the waste, the far waste of waters
And the soft lashing of black waves
For long and in loneliness.

Remember, thou, o ship of love
Thou leaves! a far waste of waters
And the soft lashing of black waves
For long and in loneliness.

- 82 -

"I have heard the sunset song of the birches
A white melody in the silence
I have seen a quarrel of the pines.
At nightfall
The little grasses have rushed by me
With the wind men.
These things have I lived," quoth the maniac,
"Possessing only eyes and ears.
But, you –
You don green spectacles before you look at roses."

- 83 -

Fast rode the knight
With spurs, hot and reeking
Ever waving an eager sword.
    "To save my lady!"
Fast rode the knight
And leaped from saddle to war.
Men of steel flickered and gleamed
Like riot of silver lights
And the gold of the knight's good banner
Still waved on a castle wall.

* * * * * * * * * * * * * * ** * *

A horse
Blowing, staggering, bloody thing
Forgotten at foot of castle wall.
A horse
Dead at foot of castle wall.

- 84 -

Forth went the candid man
And spoke freely to the wind —
When he looked about him he was in far strange country.

Forth went the candid man
And spoke freely to the stars —
Yellow light tore sight from his eyes.

"My good fool," said a learned bystander,
"Your operations are mad."

"You are too candid," cried the candid man
And when his stick left the head of the bystander
It was two sticks.

- 85 -

You tell me this is God?
I tell you this is a printed list,
A burning candle and an ass.

- 86 -

On the desert
A silence from the moon's deepest valley.
Fire-rays fall athwart the robes
Of hooded men, squat and dumb.
Before them, a woman
Moves to the blowing of shrill whistles
And distant-thunder of drums
While slow things, sinuous, dull with terrible color
Sleepily fondle her body
Or move at her will, swishing stealthily over the sand.
The snakes whisper softly;
The whispering, whispering snakes
Dreaming and swaying and staring
But always whispering, softly whispering.
The wind streams from the lone reaches
Of Arabia, solemn with night,
And the wild fire makes shimmer of blood
Over the robes of the hooded men
Squat and dumb.
Bands of moving bronze, emerald, yellow
Circle the throat and the arms of her
And over the sands serpents move warily
Slow, menacing and submissive,
Swinging to the whistles and drums,
The whispering, whispering snake,
Dreaming and swaying and staring
But always whispering, softly whispering.
The dignity of the accursed;
The glory of slavery, despair, death
Is in the dance of the whispering snakes.

- 87 -

A newspaper is a collection of half-injustices
Which, bawled by boys from mile to mile,
Spreads its curious opinion
To a million merciful and sneering men.
While families cuddle the joys of the fireside
When spurred by tale of dire lone agony.
A newspaper is a court
Where every one is kindly and unfairly tried
By a squalor of honest men.
A newspaper is a market
Where wisdom sells its freedom
And melons are crowned by the crowd.
A newspaper is a game
Where his error scores the player victory
While another's skill wins death.
A newspaper is a symbol;
It is fetless life's chronicle,
A collection of loud tales
Concentrating eternal stupidities,
That in remote ages lived unhaltered,
Roaming through a fenceless world.

- 88 -

The wayfarer
Perceiving the pathway to truth
Was struck with astonishment.
It was thickly grown with weeds.
"Ha," he said,
"I see that none has passed here
In a long time."
Later he saw that each weed
Was a singular knife.
"Well," he mumbled at last,
"Doubtless there are other roads."

- 89 -

A slant of sun on dull brown walls
A forgotten sky of bashful blue.
Toward God a mighty hymn
A song of collisions and cries
Rumbling wheels, hoof-beats, bells,
Welcomes, farewells, love-calls, final moans,
Voices of joy, idiocy, warning, despair,
The unknown appeals of brutes,
The chanting of flowers
The screams of cut trees,
The senseless babble of hens and wise men –
A cluttered incoherency that says at the stars:
"Oh, God, save us."

- 90 -

Once, a man, clambering to the house-tops,
Appealed to the heavens.
With strong voice he called to the deaf spheres;
A warrior's shout he raised to the suns.
Lo, at last, there was a dot on the clouds,
And – at last and at last –
– God – the sky was filled with armies.

- 91 -

There was a man with tongue of wood
Who essayed to sing,
And in truth it was lamentable
But there was one who heard
The clip-clapper of this tongue of wood
And knew what the man
Wished to sing,
And with that the singer was content.

- 92 -

The successful man has thrust himself
Through the water of the years,
Reeking wet with mistakes,
Bloody mistakes;
Slimed with victories over the lesser
A figure thankful on the shore of money.
Then, with the bones of fools
He buys silken banners
Limned with his triumphant face,
With the skins of wise men
He buys the trivial bows of all.
Flesh painted with marrow
Contributes a coverlet
A coverlet for his contented slumber
In guiltless ignorance, in ignorant guilt
He delivers his secrets to the riven multitude.
"Thus I defended: Thus I wrought."
Complacent, smiling
He stands heavily on the dead.
Erect on a pillar of skulls
He declaims his trampling of babes;
Smirking, fat, dripping
He makes his speech in guiltless ignorance,
Innocence.

\- 93 -

In the night
Grey, heavy clouds muffled the valleys,
And the peaks looked toward God, alone.
   "Oh, Master that movest the wind with a finger,
   Humble, idle, futile peaks are we.
   Grant that we may run swiftly across the world
   To huddle in worship at Thy feet."

In the morning
A noise of men at work came the clear blue miles
And the little black cities were apparent.
   "Oh, Master that knowest the meaning of rain –
   Humble, idle, futile peaks are we.
   Give voice to us, we pray, O Lord,
   That we may sing Thy goodness to the sun."

In the evening
The far valleys were sprinkled with tiny lights.
   "Oh, Master,
   Thou who knowest the value of kings and birds,
   Thou hast made us humble, idle, futile peaks.
   Thou only needest eternal patience;
   We bow to Thy wisdom, O Lord –
   Humble, idle, futile peaks."

In the night
Grey, heavy clouds muffled the valleys
And the peaks looked toward God, alone.

- 94 -

The chatter of a death-demon from a tree-top.

Blood-blood and torn grass —
Had marked the rise of his agony —
This lone hunter.
The grey-green woods impassive
Had watched the threshing of his limbs.

A canoe with flashing paddle
A girl with soft searching eyes,
A call: "John!"

* * * * * * * * * * * * * * * ** * * *

Come, arise, hunter!
Can you not hear?

The chatter of a death-demon from a tree-top.

- 95 -

The impact of a dollar upon the heart
Smiles warm red light
Sweeping from the hearth rosily upon the white table,
With the hanging cool velvet shadows
Moving softly upon the door.

The impact of a million dollars
Is a crash of flunkeys
And yawning emblems of Persia
Cheeked against oak, France and a sabre,
The outcry of old beauty
Whored by pimping merchants
To submission before wine and chatter.
Silly rich peasants stamp the carpets of men,
Dead men who dreamed fragrance and light
Into their woof, their lives;
The rug of an honest bear
Under the foot of a cryptic slave
Who speaks always of baubles,
Forgetting place, multitude, work and state,
Champing and mouthing of hats
Making ratful squeak of hats,
Hats.

- 96 -

A man said to the universe:
"Sir, I exist"
"However," replied the universe,
"The fact has not created in me
A sense of obligation."

- 97 -

When the prophet, a complacent fat man,
Arrived at the mountain-top
He cried: "Woe to my knowledge!
I intended to see good white lands
And bad black lands –
But the scene is grey."

- 98 -

There was a land where lived no violets.
A traveller at once demanded: "Why?"
The people told him:
"Once the violets of this place spoke thus:
"Until some woman freely gives her lover
To another woman
We will fight in bloody scuffle."
Sadly the people added:
"There are no violets here."

No 99: see No 33. Crane included the poem in both collections.

- 100 -

Aye, workman, make me a dream
A dream for my love.
Cunningly weave sunlight,
Breezes and flowers.
Let it be of the cloth of meadows.
And – good workman –
And let there be a man walking thereon.

- 101 -

Each small gleam was a voice
– A lantern voice –
In little songs of carmine, violet, green, gold.
A chorus of colors came over the water;
The wondrous leaf shadow no longer wavered,
No pines crooned on the hills
The blue night was elsewhere a silence
When the chorus of colors came over the water,
Little songs of carmine, violet, green, gold.

Small glowing pebbles
Thrown on the dark plane of evening
Sing good ballads of God
And eternity, with soul's rest.
Little priests, little holy fathers
None can doubt the truth of your hymning
When the marvelous chorus comes over the water
Songs of carmine, violet, green, gold.

- 102 -

The trees in the garden rained flowers.
Children ran there joyously.
They gathered the flowers
Each to himself.
Now there were some
Who gathered great heaps –
– Having opportunity and skill –
Until, behold, only chance blossoms
Remained for the feeble.
Then a little spindling tutor
Ran importantly to the father, crying:
"Pray, come hither!
See this unjust thing in your garden!"
But when the father had surveyed,
He admonished the tutor:
"Not so, small sage!
This thing is just.
For, look you,
Are not they who possess the flowers
Stronger, bolder, shrewder
Than they who have none?
Why should the strong –
– The beautiful strong –
Why should they not have the flowers?"

Upon reflection, the tutor bowed to the ground.
"My Lord," he said,
"The stars are misplaced
By this towering wisdom."

Intrigue

Thou art my love
And thou art the peace of sundown
When the blue shadows soothe
And the grasses and the leaves sleep
To the song of the little brooks
Woe is me.

Thou art my love
And thou art a storm
That breaks black in the sky
And, sweeping headlong,
Drenches and cowers each tree
And at the panting end
There is no sound
Save the melancholy cry of a single owl
Woe is me!

Thou art my love
And thou art a tinsel thing
And I in my play
Broke thee easily
And from the little fragments
Arose my long sorrow
Woe is me

Thou art my love
And thou art a weary violet
Drooping from sun-caresses.
Answering mine carelessly

Woe is me.

Thou art my love
And thou art the ashes of other men's love
And I bury my face in these ashes
And I love them
Woe is me.

Thou art my love
And thou art the beard
On another man's face
Woe is me.

Thou art my love
And thou art a temple
And in this temple is an altar
And on this altar is my heart
Woe is me.

Thou art my love
And thou art a wretch.
Let these sacred love-lies choke thee
For I am come to where I know your lies as truth
And your truth as lies
Woe is me.

Thou art my love
And thou art a priestess
And in thy hand is a bloody dagger
And my doom comes to me surely
Woe is me.

Thou art my love
And thou art a skull with ruby eyes
And I love thee
Woe is me.

Thou art my love
And I doubt thee
And if peace came with thy murder
Then would I murder.
Woe is me.

Thou art my love
And thou art death
Aye, thou art death
Black and yet black
But I love thee
I love thee
Woe, welcome woe, to me.

– 104 –

Love forgive me if I wish you grief
For in your grief
You huddle to my breast
And for it
Would I pay the price of your grief

You walk among men
And all men do not surrender
And this I understand
That love reaches his hand
In mercy to me.

He had your picture in his room
A scurvy traitor picture
And he smiled
– Merely a fat complacence
Of men who know fine women –
And thus I divided with him
A part of my love

Fool, not to know that thy little shoe
Can make men weep!
– Some men weep.
I weep and I gnash
And I love the little shoe
The little, little shoe.

God give me medals
God give me loud honors
That I may strut before you, sweetheart

And be worthy of –
– The love I bear you.

Now let me crunch you
With full weight of affrighted love
I doubted you
– I doubted you –
And in this short doubting
My love grew like a genie
For my further undoing.

Beware of my friends
Be not in speech too civil
For in all courtesy
My weak heart sees spectres,
Mists of desires
Arising from the lips of my chosen
Be not civil.

The flower I gave thee once
Was incident to a stride
A detail of a gesture
But search those pale petals
And see engraven thereon
A record of my intention.

- 105 -

Ah, God, the way your little finger moved
As you thrust a bare arm backward
And made play with your hair
And a comb a silly gilt comb
Ah, God-that I should suffer
Because of the way a little finger moved.

- 106 -

Once I saw thee idly rocking
– Idly rocking –
And chattering girlishly to other girls,
Bell-voiced, happy,
Careless with the stout heart of unscarred womanhood
And life to thee was all light melody.
I thought of the great storms of love as I know it
Tom, miserable and ashamed of my open sorrow,
I thought of the thunders that lived in my head
And I wish to be an ogre
And hale and haul my beloved to a castle
And there use the happy cruel one cruelly
And make her mourn with my mourning

- 107 -

Tell me why, behind thee,
I see always the shadow of another lover?
Is it real
Or is this the thrice-damned memory of a better happiness?
Plague on him if he be dead
Plague on him if he be alive
A swinish numbskull
To intrude his shade
Always between me and my peace

- 108 -

And yet I have seen thee happy with me.
I am no fool
To pole stupidly into iron.
I have heard your quick breaths
And seen your arms writhe toward me;
At those times
– God help us –
I was impelled to be a grand knight
And swagger and snap my fingers,
And explain my mind finely.
Oh, lost sweetheart,
I would that I had not been a grand knight,
I said: "Sweetheart."
Thou said'st: "Sweetheart."
And we preserved an admirable mimicry
Without heeding the drip of the blood
From my heart.

- 109 -

I heard thee laugh,
And in this merriment
I defined the measure of my pain;
I knew that I was alone,
Alone with love,
Poor shivering love,
And he, little sprite,
Came to watch with me,
And at midnight
We were like two creatures by a dead camp-fire.

- 110 -

I wonder if sometimes in the dusk,
When the brave lights that gild thy evenings
Have not yet been touched with flame,
I wonder if sometimes in the dusk
Thou rememberest a time,
A time when thou loved me
And our love was to thee all?
Is the memory rubbish now?
An old gown
Worn in an age of other fashions?
Woe is me, oh, lost one,
For that love is now to me
A supernal dream,
White, white, white with many suns.

- 111 -

Love met me at noonday,
– Reckless imp,
To leave his shaded nights
And brave the glare, –
And I saw him then plainly
For a bungler,
A stupid, simpering, eyeless bungler,
Breaking the hearts of brave people
As the sniveling idiot-boy cracks his bowl,
And I cursed him,
Cursed him to and fro, back and forth,
Into all the silly mazes of his mind,
But in the end
He laughed and pointed to my breast,
Where a heart still beat for thee, beloved.

- 112 -

I have seen thy face aflame
For love of me,
Thy fair arms go mad,
Thy lips tremble and mutter and rave.
And – surely –
This should leave a man content?
Thou lovest not me now,
But thou didst love me,
And in loving me once
Thou gavest me an eternal privilege,
For I can think of thee.

Poems Published Posthumously

A man adrift on a slim spar
A horizon smaller than the rim of a bottle
Tented waves rearing lashy dark points
The near whine of froth in circles.
                                            God is cold.

The incessant raise and swing of the sea
And growl after growl of crest
The sinkings, green, seething, endless
The upheaval half-completed.
                                            God is cold.

The seas are in the hollow of The Hand;
Oceans may be turned to a spray
Raining down through the stars
Because of a gesture of pity toward a babe.
Oceans may become grey ashes,
Die with a long moan and a roar
Amid the tumult of the fishes
And the cries of the ships,
Because The Hand beckons the mice.

A horizon smaller than a doomed assassin's cap,
Inky, surging tumults
A reeling, drunken sky and no sky
A pale hand sliding from a polished spar.
                                            God is cold.

The puff of a coat imprisoning air:
A face kissing the water-death
A weary slow sway of a lost hand
And the sea, the moving sea, the sea.
                                            God is cold.

- 114 -

Chant you loud of punishments,
Of the twisting of the heart's poor strings
Of the crash of the lightning's fierce revenge.

    Then sing I of the supple-souled men
    And the strong strong gods
    That shall meet in times hereafter
    And the amaze of the gods
    At the strength of the men.
    – The strong, strong gods –
    – And the supple-souled men –

A naked woman and a dead dwarf;
Wealth and indifference.
Poor dwarf!
Reigning with foolish kings
And dying mid bells and wine
Ending with a desperate comic palaver
While before thee and after thee
Endures the eternal clown –
– The eternal clown –
A naked woman.

- 116 -

Little birds of the night
Aye, they have much to tell
Perching there in rows
Blinking at me with their serious eyes
Recounting of flowers they have seen and loved
Of meadows and groves of the distance
And pale sands at the foot of the sea
And breezes that fly in the leaves
They are vast in experience
These little birds that come in the night.

Unwind my riddle.
Cruel as hawks the hours fly;
Wounded men seldom come home to die;
The hard waves see an arm flung high;
Scorn hits strong because of a lie;
Yet there exists a mystic tie.
Unwind my riddle.

- 118 -

Ah, haggard purse, why ope thy mouth
Like a greedy urchin
I have naught wherewith to feed thee
Thy wan checks have ne'er been puffed
Thou knowest not the fill of pride
Why then gape at me
In fashion of a wronged one
Thou do smilest wanly
And reproaches! me with thine empty stomach
Thou knowest I'd sell my steps to the grave
If t'were but honestie
Ha, leer not so,
Name me no names of wrongs committed with thee
No ghost can lay hand on thee and me
We've been too thin to do sin
What, liar? When thou was filled of gold, didst I riot?
And give thee no time to eat?
No, thou brown devil, thou art stuffed now with lies as with wealth,
The one gone to let in the other.

One came from the skies
– They said –
And with a band he bound them
A man and a woman.
Now to the man
The band was gold
And to another, iron
And to the woman, iron.
But this second man,
He took his opinion and went away
But, by heavens,
He was none too wise.

- 120 -

A god came to a man
And said to him thus:
"I have an apple
It is a glorious apple
Aye, I swear by my ancestors
Of the eternities before this eternity
It is an apple that is from
The inner thoughts of heaven's greatest.

"And this I will hang here
And then I will adjust thee here
Thus – you may reach it.
And you must stifle your nostrils
And control your hands
And your eyes
And sit for sixty years
But, – leave be the apple."

The man answered in this wise:
"Oh, most interesting God
What folly is this?
Behold, thou hast moulded my desires
Even as thou hast moulded the apple.

"How, then?
Can I conquer my life
Which is thou?
My desires?
Look you, foolish god
If I thrust behind me
Sixty white years
I am a greater god than God

And, then, complacent splendor,
Thou wilt see that the golden angels
That sing pink hymns
Around thy throne-top
Will be lower than my feet."

- 121 -

There is a grey thing that lives in the tree-tops
None know the horror of its sight
Save those who meet death in the wilderness
But one is enabled
To see branches move at its passing
To hear at times the wail of black laughter
And to come often upon mystic places
Places where the thing has just been.

If you would seek a friend among men
Remember: they are crying their wares.
If you would ask of heaven of men
Remember: they are crying their wares
If you seek the welfare of men
Remember: they are crying their wares
If you would bestow a curse upon men
Remember: they are crying their wares
    Crying their wares
    Crying their wares
If you seek the attention of men
Remember:
Help them or hinder them as they cry their wares.

- 123 -

A lad and a maid at a curve in the stream
And a shine of soft silken waters
Where the moon-beams fall through a hemlock's boughs
Oh, night dismal, night glorious.

A lad and a maid at the rail of a bridge
With two shadows adrift on the water
And the wind sings low in the grass on the shore
Oh, night dismal, night glorious.

A lad and a maid, in a canoe,
And a paddle making silver turmoil

A solder, young in years, young in ambitions
Alive as no grey-beard is alive
Laid his heart and his hopes before duty
And went staunchly into the tempest of war.
There did the bitter red winds of battle
Swirl 'gainst his youth, beat upon his ambitions,
Drink his cool clear blood of manhood
Until at coming forth time
He was alive merely as the greybeard is alive.
And for this –
The nation rendered to him a flower
A little thing – a flower
Aye, but yet not so little
For this flower grew in the nation's heart
A wet, soft blossom
From tears of her who loved her son
Even when the black battle rages
Made his face the face of furious urchin,
And this she cherished
And finally laid it upon the breast of him.
A little thing – this flower?
No – it was the flower of duty
That inhales black smoke-clouds
And fastens it's roots in bloody sod
And yet comes forth so fair, so fragrant –
It's birth is sunlight in grimmest, darkest place.

- 125 -

A row of thick pillars
Consciously bracing for the weight
Of a vanished roof
The bronze light of sunset strikes through them,
And over a floor made for slow rites.
There is no sound of singing
But, aloft, a great and terrible bird
Is watching a cur, beaten and cut,
That crawls to the cool shadows of the pillars
To die.

Oh, a rare old wine ye brewed for me
Flagons of despair
A deep deep drink of this wine of life
Flagons of despair.

    Dream of riot and blood and screams
    The rolling white eyes of dying men
    The terrible heedless courage of babes

- 127 -

There exists the eternal fact of conflict
And – next – a mere sense of locality
Afterward we derive sustenance from the winds.
Afterward we grip upon this sense of locality.
Afterward, we become patriots.
The godly vice of patriotism makes us slaves,
And – let us surrender to this falsity
Let us be patriots

Then welcome us the practical men
Thrumming on a thousand drums
The practical men, God help us.
  They cry aloud to be led to war
  Ah –
  They have been poltroons on a thousand fields
  And the sacked sad city of New York is their record
  Furious to face the Spaniard, these people, and
    crawling worms before their task
  They name serfs and send charity in bulk to better men
  They play at being free, these people of New York
  Who are too well-dressed to protest against infamy

On the brown trail
We hear the grind of your carts
To our villages,
Laden with food
Laden with food
We know you are come to our help
But –
Why do you impress upon is
Your foreign happiness?
We know it not.
(Hark!
Carts laden with food
Laden with food)
We weep because we don't understand
But your gifts form into a yoke
The food turns into a yoke
(Hark!
Carts laden with food
Laden with food)
It is our mission to vanish
Grateful because of full mouths
Destiny – Darkness
Time understands
And ye – ye bigoted men of a moment –
– Wait –
Await your turn.

All-feeling God, hear in the war-night
The rolling voices of a nation;
Through dusky billows of darkness
See the flash, the under-light, of bared swords –
– Whirling gleams like wee shells
Deep in the streams of the universe –
Bend and see a people, O, God,
A people rebuked, accursed,
By him of the many lungs
And by him of the bruised weary war-drum
(The chanting disintegrate and the two-faced eagle)
Bend and mark our steps, O, God.
Mark well, mark well,
     Father of the Never-Ending Circles
And if the path, the new path, lead awry
Then in the forest of the lost standards
Suffer us to grope and bleed apace
For the wisdom is thine.
Bend and see a people, O, God,
A people applauded, acclaimed,
By him of the raw red shoulders
The manacle-marked, the thin victim
(He lies white amid the smoking cane)
– And if the path, the path, leads straight –
Then – O, God – then bare the great bronze arm;
Swing high the blaze of the chained stars
And let look and heed
(The chanting disintegrate and the two-faced eagle)
For we go, we go in a lunge of a long blue corps
And – to Thee we commit our lifeless sons,
The convulsed and furious dead.
(They shall be white amid the smoking cane)

For, the seas shall not bar us;
The capped mountains shall not hold us back
We shall sweep and swarm through jungle and pool,
Then let the savage one bend his high chin
To see on his breast, the sullen glow of the death-medals
For we know and we say our gift.
His prize is death, deep doom.
(He shall be white amid smoking cane)

- 130 -

A grey and boiling street
Alive with rickety noise.
Suddenly, a hearse,
Trailed by black carriages
Takes a deliberate way
Through this chasm of commerce;
And children look eagerly
To find the misery behind the shades.
Hired men, impatient, drive with a longing
To reach quickly the grave-side, the end of solemnity.

Yes, let us have it over.
Drive, man, drive.
Flog your sleek-hided beasts,
Gallop – gallop – gallop.
Let us finish it quickly.

Bottles and bottles and bottles
In a merry den
And the man smiles of women
Untruthing license and joy.
Countless lights
Making oblique and confusing multiplication
In mirrors
And the light returns again to the faces.

* * * * * * * * * * * * * * *

A cellar, and a death-pale child.
A woman
Ministering commonly, degradedly,
Without manners.
A murmur and a silence
Or silence and a murmur
And then a finished silence.
The moon beams practically upon the cheap bed.

An hour, with its million trinkets of joy or pain,
Matters little in cellar or merry den
Since all is death.

intermingled,
There come in wild revelling strains
Black words, stinging
That murder flowers
The horror of profane speculation.

- 133 -

The patent of a lord
And the bangle of a bandit
Make argument
Which God solves
Only after lighting more candles.

- 134 -

Tell me not in joyous numbers
We can make our lives sublime
By – well, at least, not by
Dabbling much in rhyme.

- 135 -

My cross!

Your cross?
The real cross
Is made of pounds,
Dollars or francs.
Here I bear my palms for the silly nails
To teach the lack
– The great pain of lack –
Of coin.

Stephen Crane

Joseph Conrad

My acquaintance with Stephen Crane was brought about by Mr. Pawling, partner in the publishing firm of Mr. William Heinemann.

One day Mr. Pawling said to me: "Stephen Crane has arrived in England. I asked him if there was anybody he wanted to meet and he mentioned two names. One of them was yours." I had then just been reading, like the rest of the world, Crane's Red Badge of Courage. The subject of that story was war, from the point of view of an individual soldier's emotions. That individual (he remains nameless throughout) was interesting enough in himself, but on turning over the pages of that little book which had for the moment secured such a noisy recognition I had been even more interested in the personality of the writer. The picture of a simple and untried youth becoming through the needs of his country part of a great fighting machine was presented with an earnestness of purpose, a sense of tragic issues, and an imaginative force of expression which struck me as quite uncommon and altogether worthy of admiration.

Apparently Stephen Crane had received a favourable impression from the reading of the Nigger of the Narcissus, a book of mine which had also been published lately. I was truly pleased to hear this.

On my next visit to town we met at a lunch. I saw a young man of medium stature and slender build, with very steady, penetrating blue eyes, the eyes of a being who not only sees visions but can brood over them to some purpose.

He had indeed a wonderful power of vision, which he applied to the things of this earth and of our mortal humanity with a penetrating force that seemed to reach, within life's appearances and forms, the very spirit of life's truth. His ignorance of the world at large — he had seen very little of it —did not stand in the way of his imaginative grasp of facts, events, and picturesque men.

His manner was very quiet, his personality at first sight interesting, and he talked slowly with an intonation which on some people, mainly Americans, had, I believe, a jarring effect. But not on me. Whatever he said had a personal note, and he expressed himself with a graphic simplicity which was extremely engaging. He knew little of literature, either of his own country or of any other, but he was himself a wonderful artist in words whenever he took a pen into his hand. Then his gift came out — and it was seen then to be much more than mere felicity of language. His impressionism of phrase went really deeper than the surface. In his writing he was very sure of his effects. I don't think he was ever in doubt about what he could do. Yet it often seemed to me that he was but half aware of the exceptional quality of his achievement.

This achievement was curtailed by his early death. It was a great loss to his friends, but perhaps not so much to literature. I think that he had given his measure fully in the few books he had the time to write. Let me not be misunderstood: the loss was great, but it was the loss of the delight his art could give, not the loss of any further possible revelation. As to himself, who can say how much he gained or lost by quitting so early this world of the living, which he knew how to set before us in the terms of his own artistic vision? Perhaps he did not lose a great deal. The recognition he was accorded was rather languid and given him grudgingly. The worthiest welcome he secured for his tales in this country was from Mr. W. Henley in the New Review and later, towards the end of his life, from the late Mr. William Blackwood in his magazine. For the rest I must say that during his sojourn in England he had the misfortune to be, as the French say, *mal entouré*. He was beset by people who understood not the quality of his genius and were antagonistic to the deeper fineness of his nature. Some of them have died since, but dead or alive they are not worth speaking about now. I don't think he had any illusions about them himself: yet there was a strain of good-nature and perhaps of weakness in his character which prevented him from shaking himself free from their worthless and patronising attentions, which in those days caused me much secret irritation whenever I stayed with him in either of his English homes. My wife and I like best to remember him riding to meet us at the gate of the Park at Brede. Born master of his sincere impressions, he was also a born horseman. He never appeared so happy or so much to advantage as on the back of a horse. He had formed the project of teaching my eldest boy to ride, and meantime, when the child was about two years old, presented him with his first dog.

I saw Stephen Crane a few days after his arrival in London. I saw him for the last time on his last day in England. It was in Dover, in a big hotel, in a bedroom with a large window looking on to the sea. He had been very ill and Mrs. Crane was taking him to some place in Germany, but one glance at that wasted face was enough to tell me that it was the most forlorn of all hopes. The last words he breathed out to me were: "I am tired. Give my love to your wife and child." When I stopped at the door for another look I saw that he had turned his head on the pillow and was staring wistfully out of the window at the sails of a cutter yacht that glided slowly across the frame, like a dim shadow against the grey sky.

Those who have read his little tale, "Horses," and the story, "The Open Boat," in the volume of that name, know with what fine understanding he loved horses and the sea. And his passage on this earth was like that of a horseman riding swiftly in the dawn of a day fated to be short and without sunshine.

A note without date, 1919. From Notes on Live and Letters, Joseph Conrad, 1921.

Index of First Lines

Following the first lines of the poems are the poem numbers.

A god came to a man, 120
A god in wrath, 19
A grey and boiling street, 130
A lad and a maid at a curve in the stream, 123
A learned man came to me once, 20
A little ink more or less, 79
A man adrift on a slim spar, 113
A man built a bugle for the storms to blow, 69
A man feared that he might find an assassin, 56
A man said: "Thou tree", 71
A man said to the universe, 96
A man saw a ball of gold in the sky, 35
A man toiled on a burning road, 55
A man went before a strange god, 51
A naked woman and a dead dwarf, 115
A newspaper is a collection of half-injustices, 87
A row of thick pillars, 125
A slant of sun on dull brown walls, 89
A solder, young in years, young in ambitions, 124
A spirit sped, 68
A warrior stood upon a peak and defied the stars, 72
A youth in apparel that glittered, 27
Ah, God, the way your little finger moved, 105
Ah, haggard purse, why ope thy mouth, 118
All-feeling God, hear in the war-night, 129
And yet I have seen thee happy with me, 108
And you love me, 40
Aye, workman, make me a dream, 100
Behold, from the land of the farther suns, 29
Behold, the grave of a wicked man, 25
Black Riders came from the sea, 1
Blustering god, 53
Bottles and bottles and bottles, 131
Chant you loud of punishments, 114
Charity, thou art a lie, 16
Do not weep, maiden, for war is kind, 76
Each small gleam was a voice, 101
Fast rode the knight, 83
Forth went the candid man, 84
Friend, your white beard sweeps the ground, 64
God fashioned the ship of the world carefully, 6
God lay dead in Heaven, 67

"Have you ever made a just man", 80
I explain the silvered passing of a ship at night, 81
I have heard the sunset song of the birches, 82
I have seen thy face aflame, 112
I heard thee laugh, 109
I looked here, 8
I met a seer, 36
I saw a man pursuing the horizon, 24
I stood musing in a black world, 49
I stood upon a high place, 9
I stood upon a highway, 34
I walked in a desert, 42
I was in the darkness, 44
I wonder if sometimes in the dusk, 110
If I should cast off this tattered coal, 66
If there is a witness to my little life, 13
If you would seek a friend among men, 122
In a lonely place, 11
In Heaven, 18
intermingled, 132
In the desert, 3
In the night, 93
"It was wrong to do this," said the angel, 54
Little birds of the night, 116
Love forgive me if I wish you grief, 104
Love met me at noonday, 111
Love walked alone, 41
Many red devils ran from my heart, 46
Many workmen, 31
My cross, 135
Mystic Shadow, bending near me, 7
Oh, a rare old wine ye brewed for me, 126
On the brown trail, 128
On the desert, 86
On the horizon the peaks assembled, 37
Once, a man, clambering to the house-tops, 90
Once, I knew a fine song, 65
Once I saw Mountains angry, 22
Once I saw thee idly rocking, 106
Once there came a man, 5
Once there was a man, 48
One came from the skies, 119
Places among the stars, 23
Rumbling, buzzing, turning, whirling Wheels, 75
Should the wide world roll away, 10
Supposing that I should have the courage, 30
"Tell brave deeds of war", 15

Tell me not in joyous numbers, 134
The livid lightnings flashed in the clouds, 39
Tell me why, behind thee, 107
The chatter of a death-demon from a tree-top, 94
The impact of a dollar upon the heart, 95
The ocean said to me once, 38
The patent of a lord, 133
The sage lectured brilliantly, 58
The successful man has thrust himself, 92
The trees in the garden rained flowers, 102
The wayfarer, 88
The wind that waves the blossoms, 73
There came whisperings in the winds, 43
There exists the eternal fact of conflict, 127
There is a grey thing that lives in the tree-tops, 121
There was a great cathedral, 63
There was a land where lived no violets, 98
There was a man and a woman, 61
There was a man who lived a life of fire, 62
There was a man with tongue of wood, 91
There was, before me, 21
There was crimson clash of war, 14
There was one I met upon the road, 33
There was set before me a mighty hill, 26
There were many who went in huddled procession, 17
"Think as I think," said a man, 47
Thou art my love, 103
Three little birds in a row, 2
To the maiden, 78
Tradition, thou art for suckling children, 45
"Truth," said a traveller, 28
Two or three angels, 32
The sage lectured brilliantly, 59
Unwind my riddle, 117
Upon the road of my life, 60
Well, then, I hate Thee, Unrighteous Picture, 12
What says the sea, little shell, 77
When a people reach the top of a hill, 74
When the prophet, a complacent fat man, 97
When the suicide arrived at the sky, the people, 70
Why do you strive for greatness, fool, 52
With eye and with gesture, 57
Yes, I have a thousand tongues, 4
You say you are holy, 50
You tell me this is God, 85

Other books published by Honeycomb Press:

Stephen Crane. The O'Ruddy. A Romance
(ISBN 978-1-4478-2608-8)

Ethel Lilian Voynich. The Gadfly. A Novel
(ISBN 978-1-4478-3375-8)

Karl Gjellerup. Minna. A Novel
translated from Danish
(ISBN 978-1-4478-6746-3)

Anatoly Kudryavitsky. Dream. After Dream. Novellas
translated from Russian
(ISBN 978-1-4478-6503-2)

Our books are available to order via
http://honeycombpress.webs.com,
or via http://www.lulu.com/spotlight/Honeycomb

Printed in Great Britain
by Amazon